My spot

Dad hopped up out of his chair to get a cup of coffee.

He got back and Pam was in his spot. She wagged her tail.

That's my spot!

Nat entered her bedroom.
Pam was napping in the
doll's pram.

"You are far too big for that spot, Pam!" said Nat. Pam seemed to grin.

Dan looked at Sid's
bed. Pam was in it.

Dan said, "You had better hop out, Pam. Sid will get cross if he sees you in his spot."

Sam was chilling out in the hammock. Pam jumped up next to him.

"There is no room, Pam.
This is my spot!" said Sam.

Pam was resting on the back step in the sun. "This is not a good spot, Pam. It is hard for us to get in and out," said Dad.

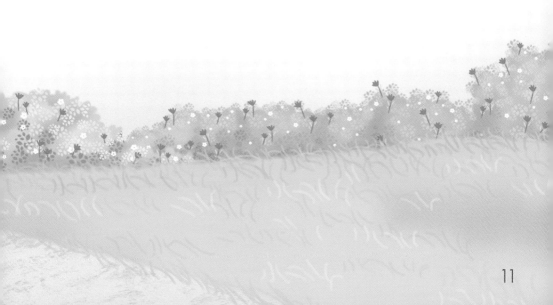

That night, Mum went to get into bed but there was Pam on the quilt!
"No, Pam! Get off!" said Mum.
Pam licked her cheek.

The next morning, Mum
got back from the pet
shop. She had the biggest,
softest bed for Pam.

Pam flopped right on to it and wagged her tail!

Pam thinks that her spot is
the best.

Words to blend

looked	good	bedroom
tail	room	chair
coffee	seemed	cheek
tail	entered	better
far	hard	morning
flopped	for	softest
just	twists	pram

Before reading

Synopsis: Pam likes to sleep anywhere but she especially likes to sleep on a chair, in a pram, on a bed, in a hammock and in Sid's bed. This isn't popular with the family!

Review graphemes/phonemes: oo oo air ee ai er ar or

Story discussion: Look at the cover and read the title together. Ask: *Who do you think this story is going to be about? Do you have a spot where you live that you think of as being your spot?*

Link to prior learning: Display a word with adjacent consonants from the story, e.g. *resting*. Ask children to put a dot under each single-letter grapheme (*r, e, s, t, i*) and a line under the digraph (*ng*). Model, if necessary, how to sound out and blend the adjacent consonants together to read the word. Repeat with another word from the story, e.g. *softest*, and encourage children to sound out and blend the word independently.

Vocabulary check: quilt – a soft, thick cover for a bed

Decoding practice: Turn to page 7. Point to the words *cross* and *spot* and check that children can sound out and blend them.

Tricky word practice: Display the word *my*. Read the word, and ask children to show you the tricky bit (*y*, which makes the sound /igh/). Practise reading and spelling the word.

After reading

Apply learning: Ask: *Can you retell the story in your own words?* Try to remember all the places Pam went to. Children can look back at the book if they need help.

Comprehension

- Why did Dan tell Pam to hop out of Sid's bed?

- How did Sam feel about Pam trying to share the hammock with him?

- What was Pam's own spot, in the end?

Fluency

- Pick a page that most of the group read quite easily. Ask them to reread it with pace and expression. Model how to do this if necessary.

- Encourage children to read Dad's words on page 11, with as much expression as they can.

- Practise reading the words on page 17.

Tricky words review

my	out	was
she	you	are
he	into	said
her	no	there
of	the	we